Survivor

Your Past Doesn't Define You

Based on a True Story

Anthony J Placito

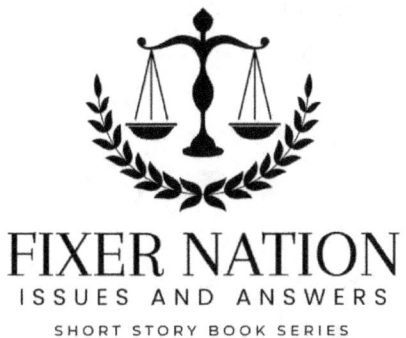

FIXER NATION

ISSUES AND ANSWERS

SHORT STORY BOOK SERIES

Our Mission

Fixer Nation (FN) is your modern-day source for clear, reliable solutions to everyday questions and challenges. Whether you're facing a dilemma or seeking clarity on an issue, Fixer Nation provides unbiased insights, practical tools, and valuable resources to help you find the right answers—and discover who or what can truly be the Fixer in your situation.

Our Vision

Fixer Nation (FN) will be the leading global platform for positivity, health, and wellness—uniquely designed to help every member navigate life's challenges, achieve their goals, and feel genuinely supported. Not everyone is welcome—only those ready to rise.

We envision a world where personal transformation is powered by collective strength, and every individual feels empowered to break through their barriers.

Our Values

At Fixer Nation, we believe in empowering individuals through guidance and support. We lead with positivity, prioritize purpose over popularity, and foster a safe, judgment-free space. Every journey is personal, so we tailor content to your unique goals—while cultivating a high-standard community focused on authentic growth.

FIXER NATION

POSITIVITY, HEALTH, AND WELLNESS

Congratulations on Investing in Yourself!
Welcome to Fixer Nation — The Health Club for Your
Mind, Body & Soul

You've taken a powerful step forward by joining the Fixer Nation community and purchasing your book — your personal guide to turning life's issues into answers.

Now it's time to activate your FREE 90-day membership inside Fixer Nation: The Positivity, Health, and Wellness Network. The health club for your mind, body and soul.

A Health Club Like No Other
This isn't just another program — it's a movement.

Fixer Nation is where positivity meets purpose, where personal growth meets daily action, and where your best self takes center stage.

Your journey begins with our exclusive Morning Boost — 7 Daily Success Rituals that help you:

☑ Strengthen your mindset and emotional resilience
☑ Fuel your body with purpose and positivity
☑ Build lasting gratitude, focus, and confidence

☑ Create habits that lead to success and joy
☑ Connect with a community that lifts you higher every day

⚡ Your Morning Boost Experience

Each day, you'll receive inspiration, humor, reflection, and action

— everything you need to align your mind, body, and soul with your highest potential.

This is where small steps become big breakthroughs — where you learn to live intentionally and joyfully.

Your 90-Day Free Membership Includes

✴ Daily Morning Boost (7 Success Rituals)
✴ Exclusive Fixer Nation Content Library
✴ Health & Wellness Tools for Body and Mind
✴ Access to the Fixer Nation Positivity Community

💬 What Members Say

"This changed my mornings — and my mindset."
"Fixer Nation reminds me daily that I have what it takes."

💪 You Were Born a Fixer — You Just Don't Know It Yet

Your book opened the door — now this 90-day experience will show you what's possible when positivity becomes your lifestyle.

🚀 Start Your Journey Today

You've already made the investment in yourself.

Now claim what you've earned — your 90 days of growth, clarity, and empowerment.

👉 **[Scan the QR Code and enter coupon code 90dayfreetrial to Start Your Free 90 Days]**

Your transformation begins now — only at **Fixer Nation: The Positivity, Health & Wellness Network- Welcome to your Health Club for Your Mind, Body and Soul**

Acknowledgments

This project has been a significant undertaking, and I am deeply grateful for the support and encouragement of the many individuals who made it possible. I would like to extend my sincere thanks to all of you.

It has been an honor and a privilege to work with the Fixer Nation Business Development Services Team. I sincerely thank them for their guidance, constant supervision, and invaluable insights throughout this process. Their willingness to share their vast knowledge helped me gain a deeper understanding of the project and its complexities, ultimately enabling me to excel and succeed.

I would also like to express my heartfelt gratitude to my parents, family members, and friends for their unwavering support, encouragement, and guidance throughout my journey. Their belief in me has been instrumental in the successful completion of this stage of my ongoing journey.

Finally, my appreciation extends to my colleagues and everyone who has generously shared their time, expertise, and efforts in bringing this project to fruition. Your contributions have been invaluable, and I am truly grateful.

Dedication

This book is dedicated to you, the reader.

If you have a problem, you've come to the right place to solve it.

FIXER NATION *CREDO:

We believe there are no problems in life—only issues and answers.

You are *"The Fixer"*—and together, *We are "Fixer Nation"*.

Fixer Nation was created for you and it's more than a social media platform—it's a community designed to help people become the best versions of themselves.

Our network connects like-minded, goal-oriented individuals who are committed to improving their lives with the people, companies, and tools that can assist them on their journey toward achieving their goals.

Fixer Nation is your community where real people engage in real discussions about positivity, health, and personal growth. This is a space for those who want to excel, not just exist.

It is the premier community for those committed to thriving in life.

We are Fixer Nation!

Credo - *A set of beliefs that influences the way you live.*

About the Author

With 25 years of experience in the education market, Anthony J. Placito has dedicated his career to providing technology-driven solutions for schools, developing curricula for students from kindergarten through university.

Throughout his journey, Anthony recognized a deeper need—to offer guidance and insight into the everyday challenges people face. He believes that in life, there are no problems, only issues and answers.

Inspired by this philosophy, he created Fixer Nation – Issues & Answers, a short story series designed to engage young and mature minds alike, offering thought-provoking perspectives on life's challenges and potential solutions.

Expanding on this mission, Anthony also founded Fixer Nation – The Positivity, Health & Wellness Network, an exclusive members-only social platform dedicated to personal growth, support, and empowerment. This safe place was built to help individuals become the best version of themselves—every single day.

Welcome to Fixer Nation.

Your safe place to grow.

It was built just for you.

Cheers.

Introduction – How it All Began

Emily Turner

Growing up, I always felt like I had everything I needed. My parents, Greg and Karen, weren't rich, but they made sure our home was safe, comfortable, and filled with love. We weren't the kind of family that went on lavish vacations or had the latest gadgets, but there was always dinner on the table, clean clothes in the drawers, and a sense of stability that I never questioned.

I spent most of my time reading, writing, or tinkering with my cameras. Photography fascinated me—capturing moments, freezing time, seeing the world through different angles. It started with an old Polaroid camera Dad gave me when I was eight, and from there, I was hooked. By middle school, I had a digital camera and had figured out how to set up motion sensors and hidden lenses. I didn't just take pictures—I learned how to observe.

And then there was Sam. She was my best friend, my partner in crime, and the one person I could always count on. We spent hours at the park, riding bikes, and making up elaborate spy games using our childhood nanny cam's where we'd hide, watch, and document everything around us. It was innocent fun back then, just two kids playing detective.

But something changed when middle school started. Sam pulled away. It wasn't just the usual drifting apart that happens as kids grow up—she became distant, withdrawn. She stopped coming over, stopped answering my messages. At first, I thought she was just busy. Then, I started noticing other things—how she avoided eye contact, how she never wanted to talk about home, how she started hanging around with kids who seemed… different. Edgier.

I didn't understand. I wanted to help, but she pushed me away. So I did what I knew best—I watched. I started paying attention, not just to her but to the world around her. I noticed the way she flinched when certain people got too close. The way she always seemed to be looking over her shoulder. The way her laughter never reached her eyes anymore.

Now, at sixteen, I'm still the quiet girl with the camera, the one people don't quite understand. They call me a nerd, a loner. I don't mind. I've learned to embrace who I am. But sometimes, when I catch a glimpse of Sam in the halls, I wonder if she's okay. I wonder if she ever thinks about our old spy games.

Because now, watching and documenting things isn't just a game anymore.

It's how I see the truth.

Samantha "Sam" Miller

It's funny how life can change without you even realizing it. One minute, everything's fine, and the next, the world feels like it's crashing down around you.

I used to be happy. I used to laugh and run through the streets with Emily, my best friend, who seemed to have everything figured out. I was never jealous of her, at least not at first. I didn't care about her perfect family, her nice house, her perfect grades. I was happy with what I had, or at least, I pretended to be. But then my world started to fall apart, and it's like I didn't know how to stop it.

My dad died when I was 2; he was a cop, my mom told me. From his pictures, he seems very handsome. I wish I had known him. Currently, he is equivalent to a model in a picture for me, as that is the only place I have ever seen him. I didn't have any other family; I don't know why, but for me, my mom was everything. Unfortunately for her, that wasn't the case.

My mom, she wasn't like Emily's mom. My mom, Rachel, was a wreck. She'd drink herself to sleep most nights, and when she wasn't drunk, she was with her loser of a boyfriend. The one I had to deal with, though—he was something else. A real piece of work. He started showing up at our house when I was in middle school, and at first, it was okay. He didn't seem so bad. But then things started to change.

I don't remember exactly when it happened, but one day, he just started getting rough with me. It was subtle at first—just a shove or a harsh word here and there but then one day when he was really drunk he started to touch me, and then he did things I do not like to repeat.

3

Since then he has made that a practice. Whenever my mom's away he hounds me. Even when my mom is home he finds moments to let me know what a creep he is when my mom is not looking and let's be honest she is never looking at all at what he does.

I didn't tell anyone because I didn't know who will even be willing to listen. And I was scared. What if my mom found out? What if she kicked me out? I didn't have anywhere to go, and I couldn't imagine facing that kind of rejection.

So, I shut down. I stopped talking to Emily. I stopped being the girl who laughed with her best friend. The girl who rode bikes and talked about everything. I pulled away from her, and it hurt. But I didn't know how else to protect her from what was going on in my life. I couldn't bear to see her so happy, so perfect, while I was falling apart. So, I pushed her away. I pushed everyone away.

I started hanging out with the crowd that has seen this in their lives, the kids who didn't care about rules or consequences. They didn't ask questions, and I didn't have to pretend anymore. I didn't have to be the girl with a perfect life. I could just be numb. And it worked.

I didn't know what else to do. I couldn't go back to the girl I once was. I didn't know how. And Emily—she was just so perfect. She deserved better than me. She deserved better than the mess I had become.

Chapter 1: The Shift

Emily Turner

Senior year was shaping up exactly how I'd hoped. My classes were challenging but manageable, my college applications were almost done, and my friends were the kind of people I could count on. Life felt steady, predictable, good.

Still, there was one thing I couldn't ignore—Sam.

I wasn't naïve. People change. Friendships drift. But this felt different. Sam wasn't just distant—she was shutting me out completely. It wasn't the gradual fading of a childhood bond. It was sharp, intentional, like she wanted nothing to do with me.

At lunch, I'd catch glimpses of her sitting with her new friends— loud, reckless, the kind of people who never worried about tests or curfews. She laughed at their jokes, leaned into their chaos, but even from across the cafeteria, I could tell it wasn't real. She was playing a part.

I tried to brush it off. Maybe she was just... figuring things out. Maybe she didn't need me anymore. But something told me that wasn't it.

Sam had always been tough—louder than me, braver than me. But there was a hardness in her now, a sharp edge that hadn't been there before. The way she carried herself, the way she flinched if someone moved too fast near her. I noticed.

And maybe that was the worst part. I noticed, but I had no idea what to do.

Sam was different.

I'd always known her home life wasn't great—not because she ever told me, but because I was around her enough to see it. She never talked about it, but the signs were there.

She never let me come over. Ever. She'd make up excuses—her mom was sick, the place was a mess, she had to go somewhere— but it was clear she didn't want me near her house. And then there were the bruises. A black eye one time, a split lip another. She always brushed it off. *I fell. It's nothing.* But no one falls that many times.

Still, when we were alone, away from whatever was weighing her down, she was... brilliant. Sam had this way of making everything fun, of knowing things no one else did, like how to pick a lock with a hairpin or how to find constellations even in a light-polluted sky. She was one of the smartest people I knew. But the second it was time to go home, everything about her changed. She'd tense up, her face would shut down, and she'd leave without saying much.

I used to wonder what she was hiding. Now, I just wondered how we got here.

Because at some point, she didn't just pull away—she shut me out completely. No explanation. No fight. Just silence.

Maybe that was my answer. Maybe I wasn't meant to know. People grow, people change.

Time to focus on my life now.

Chapter 2: Jake

Emily Turner

I never expected to meet someone like Jake Whitman.

It was just another Tuesday, nothing special. I was in the library, lost in my history notes, when I heard a voice.

"Mind if I sit here?"

I looked up, and there he was—Jake. Soft brown hair, kind green eyes, the type of boy who never seemed to be in a rush. He was in my chemistry class, always sitting in the back, never drawing too much attention to himself.

"Yeah, sure," I said, moving my books aside.

For a while, neither of us spoke. I assumed he was just here to study, but then he leaned forward, glancing at my notes.

"European revolutions?" he asked.

I nodded. *"Test next week."*

"Right. I should probably be studying for that, but..." He sighed dramatically, tapping his pen against his notebook. *"History is not my strong suit."*

I smirked. *"Lucky for you, it's mine."*

His lips curled into a smile. *"You offering to tutor me, Turner?"*

"That depends," I teased. *"Are you a lost cause?"*

"Possibly," he admitted with a laugh.

It was easy talking to him. No pressure, no awkwardness. We sat there for over an hour, bouncing between history facts and random tangents—his love for old detective movies, my inability to whistle, the best places to get fries after school.

Before I knew it, the librarian was announcing closing time.

"I guess I'll see you in class," Jake said, standing up.

"Maybe you won't fail the test after all," I joked.

"Only if my tutor is as good as she claims." He grinned and walked off, leaving me staring after him.

Maybe this year wouldn't be so bad after all.

Over the next few weeks, Jake and I grew closer. We studied together, grabbed coffee after school, and sent each other ridiculous memes at midnight. He made me laugh in a way I hadn't in a long time.

For the first time in a while, I felt like someone saw me—not as the "prude" people whispered about, but as *me*.

Of course, Sam noticed.

She didn't say anything at first, just watched. But I felt the shift. Her usual passive-aggressive comments turned sharper, her stares lingered longer. One day, as I passed her locker, she leaned in just enough to be heard.

"Didn't peg you for the type to fall for some boring, nice guy."

I ignored her, but the tension between us only grew.

Then came the school event.

The fall festival was one of the biggest school events of the year. Bonfire, games, live music—it was supposed to be fun.

Jake and I had planned to go together, but when I arrived, he wasn't where we agreed to meet. Confused, I pulled out my phone.

Jake: Hey, something came up. See you later.

I frowned. Something felt *off.*

As I made my way through the crowd, I spotted Sam—right next to Jake. She was laughing, her hand casually resting on his arm. My stomach twisted.

I approached, forcing a smile. *"Hey, Jake."*

He looked up, something unreadable in his expression. *"Hey, Emily."*

I glanced at Sam, who smirked.

"Oh, sorry, Em. I was just telling Jake how you're not really into dating," she said, tilting her head innocently. *"I mean, you've never really been interested in anyone before, so I figured you weren't into... all this."*

I blinked. *"What?"*

"Relax, it's fine," she continued. *"Jake was just saying he understands. Right, Jake?"*

He hesitated. I could see the doubt flickering in his eyes.

I turned to him. *"That's not true. Sam's twisting things."*

"It's okay, Emily," he said, but his voice lacked conviction. *"I just... I don't want to pressure you if you're not interested."*

I felt my chest tighten. Sam had done what she always did—made me look like something I wasn't.

Before I could say anything else, she looped her arm through Jake's. *"Anyway, we should go. The bonfire's starting."*

Jake gave me one last uncertain glance before letting her pull him away.

I stood there, heart pounding, feeling like I'd just lost something I hadn't even fully had yet.

I walked aimlessly through the festival, the sounds of laughter and music blurring around me. My chest felt tight, my hands clenched into fists at my sides. I couldn't believe Sam had done this—again.

Jake had looked at me like I was someone he *had* to let go of, not someone he *wanted* to stay. And Sam? She had smiled through it all, acting as if she hadn't just destroyed something that meant so much to me.

I found an empty spot near the edge of the bonfire, away from the crowd, and sat down on the cold grass. I hated that I felt like crying. Hated that I had let myself think, even for a second, that Jake could be different.

"Wow. You're still crying over her?"

I wiped my face quickly and looked up to see Alina, arms crossed, staring down at me with a mix of annoyance and pity.

"What do you want?" I asked, voice hoarse.

She sighed, sitting down beside me. *"Look, I don't get why you even care about Sam anymore. She's a horrible person, Emily."*

I frowned. *"She wasn't always like this."*

Alina scoffed. *"Yeah? Well, she is now. You wanna know what she told Jake?"*

I hesitated. *"What?"*

"She told him that you've 'told everyone' how you don't want anyone. That you think relationships are pointless and that Jake was pressuring you."

My stomach dropped.

"That's not true."

"Of course it's not," Alina said, rolling her eyes. *"But that's what he believes now. And when he started feeling bad about it, guess who was right there to 'comfort' him?"*

I didn't answer. I already knew.

"Sam got close when he was vulnerable. And as you can see, she stole him away. Just like she stole your friends. You're the only one who hasn't figured out that she's not worth it."

I clenched my jaw. *"I don't need you telling me what I should or shouldn't feel."*

Alina threw her hands up. *"Fine. Keep hurting yourself over someone who clearly doesn't care about you. But don't say I didn't warn you."*

She stood up, brushing off her jeans, and walked away.

I stayed there, staring at the fire, trying to swallow the lump in my throat.

Maybe Alina was right. Maybe it was time to stop caring.

Chapter 3: Sam's Darkness

Samantha "Sam" Miller

I push open the door, the hinges groaning like they're just as tired of this place as I am. The house smells like stale beer and cigarette smoke, and the lights are off except for the faint glow from the kitchen. Mom's probably passed out.

I know I did the right thing.

Emily doesn't see it yet, but I'm saving her.

Jake might seem sweet now, but they all do at first. They smile, say the right things, make you feel safe. But in the end, all they want is to use you and throw you away. That's what men do. That's what *people* do.

I'm already broken. Maybe I can protect my friend in this twisted way.

"Where have you been?"

His voice comes from the living room, thick with alcohol and something worse.

I don't answer. I just keep walking, hoping if I don't look at him, he'll let it go.

But I should know better by now.

He grabs my arm, yanking me back so hard I stumble.

"I asked you a question."

His breath is hot, reeking of whiskey and cigarettes. My stomach turns.

"Out," I mutter.

His grip tightens. *"When I need you, you're here. Do you understand me?"*

I nod, biting the inside of my cheek so hard I taste blood.

But he isn't done. His other hand moves, fingers digging into my side. *"But now I'm tired. You missed your chance to be useful."*

The words make my skin crawl. Then—

The first hit. A slap across my face, sharp and fast, sending me reeling.

Then another. A fist to my ribs.

I don't cry. I don't fight. I just take it.

When he finally lets go, I don't move, don't breathe, until I hear the front door slam.

He's gone. Off to some bar.

I sink to the floor, curling into myself, my whole body shaking.

I did the right thing.

I saved Emily.

I tell myself that over and over, hoping it'll make the pain go away.

Chapter 4: Over the Limit

Emily Turner

I see her the next morning, standing by her locker like nothing happened. Like she didn't rip my heart out the night before. My hands clench into fists at my sides. I want to march over there, demand answers, scream in her face, anything to make her feel even a fraction of the pain she's put me through. But then I see it—the black eye. A fresh one.

My anger wavers for a second.

Did she mess with someone else's boyfriend, too? Did she push the wrong girl this time? It wouldn't surprise me. Sam's been on a warpath lately, burning bridges, wrecking everything in her way. And me? I was just another casualty.

I force myself to look away. I can't care anymore. I won't.

Then I see Jake.

He's walking down the hall, head low, hands shoved in his pockets. I swallow, forcing down the lump in my throat, and muster up a small, hesitant "Hey."

He stops, glances at me, and for a moment, I think maybe—maybe—he'll say something. Maybe he'll explain. Maybe this is all some kind of misunderstanding.

But he just gives me a shy wave and walks past me. Right to Sam.

I can't breathe.

My fingers tighten around the strap of my bag as I watch them. Sam leans against the lockers, acting like she doesn't have a care in the world. Jake shifts nervously beside her, rubbing the back of his neck. She says something, and he actually smiles.

I turn away.

I shouldn't care. I should be furious. I should be done. But the ache in my chest tells me otherwise.

The day drags on. Every class is a blur of words I barely register. My friends notice something's wrong, but I shake them off with forced smiles and half-hearted excuses. I just want to get through the day without breaking.

Then the final bell rings.

I head to the parking lot, hoping to escape before I have to see them again. But of course, the universe has other plans.

I hear laughter—hers. I stop. Turn.

Sam is standing by the old oak tree near the edge of the lot. Jake is with her.

My Jake.

No. Not mine. Not anymore.

I take a step closer, heart pounding.

Then it happens.

Sam glances at me, just for a second. Just long enough to make sure I'm watching.

Then she grabs Jake by the collar of his jacket, pulls him in, and kisses him.

My stomach drops.

I can't move.

Jake hesitates—just for a second—but then he kisses her back.

And just like that, whatever hope I had left shatters.

The world spins, my breath coming in short, shallow gasps. A sharp, painful lump forms in my throat, but I refuse to cry. Not here. Not in front of her.

I force my feet to move, stumbling back, then turning away. I don't know where I'm going. I just need to get away.

But then I hear her voice.

"You don't own him, Emily."

I stop. My hands tremble at my sides.

"You never wanted him, anyway."

I spin around so fast I nearly lose my balance.

"You don't get to say that," I snap. My voice is shaking, but I don't care. "You don't get to decide what I feel."

Sam crosses her arms, tilting her head. "I just made it easier for you. You were always so scared of love. Of getting close to someone. Now you don't have to worry about it."

Something inside me snaps.

"You think you're helping me?" My voice rises. "You humiliated me. You took everything from me—" My breath catches. "You stole my first—" I can't even say it. The words feel like broken glass on my tongue.

Sam's smirk fades for just a second.

She looks away. "First kiss isn't that big of a deal, Em."

I let out a bitter laugh. "It was to me."

Silence.

Something flickers across her face—guilt, maybe? I don't know, and I don't care.

I take a step forward, voice low but sharp. "I don't know what happened to you, Sam. But this? Whatever this is? It's not friendship. It's not even hate. It's just cruel."

She flinches.

Good.

I turn on my heel and walk away.

This time, I don't look back.

Chapter 5: Sam's Secret

Emily Turner

I have never been this angry before.

It's a rage that burns hot and bright, consuming every rational thought. It's in the way my hands shake, the way my breath comes fast and shallow, the way my heart pounds so hard it might burst from my chest.

I want to hurt her. I want to make her feel even a fraction of the pain she's put me through.

So I take a rock.

I grip it so tightly my knuckles turn white. I don't care if it's stupid, if it's reckless, if it's completely unlike me.

I just want her to suffer.

The streets blur as I walk. By the time I reach her house, the sky is dark, and my anger has only grown. I stand outside the weathered home, my pulse thrumming in my ears. The place looks as run-down as I remember—peeling paint, sagging porch, a broken front step no one has bothered to fix.

I could throw the rock from here. But no. That's not enough.

I spot the tree near her window. I remember climbing it when we were kids, sneaking in and out when Sam's mom wasn't home.

Clenching my jaw, I start climbing.

The bark scrapes my palms, but I barely feel it. My fingers tremble, not from nerves, but from the raw, unrelenting anger burning inside me. When I reach a thick branch near her window, I balance myself, pulling the rock from my pocket.

One throw. Just one.

But then I see it.

The room is dimly lit, the curtains barely parted. Sam is standing inside, her posture stiff, her arms wrapped around herself like she's trying to disappear.

And then I see him.

Her mother's boyfriend.

He's standing too close.

I freeze, fingers gripping the rough bark.

At first, he's gentle—too gentle. He places a hand on her shoulder, tilting his head like he's sorry for something. Sam doesn't move. She just stares at the floor, motionless.

Then he cups her cheek.

I suck in a sharp breath.

Sam flinches but doesn't pull away.

He says something I can't hear. His lips move, his expression soft, coaxing. An apology? A lie?

She doesn't react.

Then, slowly, his hand slides down to her arm.

Sam stiffens.

She says something—something small, hesitant. A plea.

His expression shifts.

The fake kindness is gone, replaced by something darker.

He grabs her wrist, his grip tight. Sam doesn't fight him. She just stands there, her body tense, her breath coming fast.

Then, he leans down.

And he kisses her.

My stomach turns.

I can't move. I can't breathe.

This isn't happening.

Sam jerks back, shaking her head, whispering something, but I see the way her hands tremble, the way she curls into herself.

Then his expression changes again.

The mask slips entirely.

His grip tightens, his voice sharp, low, a threat. He raises a hand like he's going to hit her.

Sam goes still.

Then she obeys.

I want to scream.

I want to throw the rock through the window, to break down the door, to rip her away from him.

But I can't move.

The realization crashes into me all at once, drowning me in a suffocating weight.

This is why.

This is why she changed.

This is why she pushed me away, why she grew cold, why she sabotaged anything good in her life.

Because this is her life.

How long? How long has she been going through this?

How many times has she been forced to endure this?

My vision blurs. I shift, my body numb, but the branch beneath me is slick, and suddenly—

I slip.

The world tilts, and then I'm falling.

I hit the ground hard. Pain jolts up my side, but I barely register it. The impact sends a loud rustling through the bushes, a sharp noise in the quiet night.

I panic.

Above me, the window creaks open.

Then I see her.

Sam's face appears, her eyes wide, her lips parted. She looks down at me, frozen in horror.

She knows.

She knows I saw.

I scramble to my feet and run.

I don't stop. I don't look back.

I just run, my breath coming in ragged gasps, my heart pounding in my ears.

Because now, I know the truth.

And so does she.

Chapter 6: Boiling Point

Samantha "Sam" Miller

I walk into school the next day, the halls feeling like a minefield. Everyone's staring, and I can almost feel their thoughts crawling under my skin. Maybe they know. Maybe they can see what I've been hiding. But I'm not ready for that. Not yet. Not ever.

Emily's there, standing in the hall with her stupid, concerned look on her face. The one that used to make me want to punch her in the arm just to get her to stop acting so perfect. I hate that look. I hate that she actually cares.

She's been gone for years, but now, here she is. Staring at me like she knows. And she does. I can see it in her eyes. She knows what happened. Yesterday. In my room. She saw it.

"Sam," she says, voice soft, hesitant, like she's not sure if she should even approach me.

Great. Here it comes. She's going to tell. She's going to run her mouth to someone, to my mom, and then I'll lose everything. She'll ruin everything.

"Shut up, Emily," I snap, spinning around to face her. My voice is sharp, like a knife in the air. "Don't say anything. You hear me? Not a word. You don't know anything. You didn't see anything."

I'm trembling, but she can't see that. She can't see me break down. I won't let her see that side of me. I refuse.

Emily raises an eyebrow, still calm. Too calm. Like she's just waiting for me to lose it. And I do. I lose it.

"I said shut up!" My voice is louder now, more frantic. The walls are closing in on me. I feel the weight of everything—the lies, the secrets, the guilt—pressing on my chest. I try to push it down, but it's impossible. "You think you can just walk back in and be the good little saint, huh? You think you know everything because you saw one stupid thing? I don't need you. I don't need anyone."

She doesn't flinch, doesn't take a step back. If anything, she steps closer.

"You're scared," she says, voice quiet but firm. It's not a question. She's not judging. She's just stating the obvious.

"Shut up, Emily!" I shout again, but this time, my voice cracks. I hate it. I hate myself. "You think you know me? You don't know a thing about me, about my life. So just leave me alone."

She doesn't, though. She keeps standing there, just looking at me like she sees right through all the facade. It pisses me off, but it also… it hurts. It hurts more than anything else she could've said.

"Sam," she says softly, her voice breaking through the noise in my head. "You don't have to pretend anymore. You don't have to act like everything's fine. I saw what happened. I know what's going on, and I'm not going to turn my back on you. You're not alone."

I can feel my chest tightening. I want to shove her away. I want to scream at her to leave me alone, to stop looking at me like I'm some lost puppy. But instead, I just stand there, shaking, my fists clenched at my sides.

"I don't need you to feel sorry for me," I mutter, the words barely a whisper. "I don't need your pity."

"I'm not pitying you, Sam," she says, her voice so calm, so steady. It makes me want to punch something. "I'm trying to help you."

I laugh, bitter and sharp. "Help me? You think you can help me? You think you can just swoop in like some hero and fix everything?"

I look at her, really look at her, and I see the truth in her eyes. She's not scared. She's not judging me. She's offering something real, something I don't deserve. I'm not sure if I can accept it.

"You don't understand," I say, my voice trembling. "You don't know what it's like… I can't tell anyone. I can't tell my mom what he's been doing. If she finds out…" I feel the knot in my throat tightening. "I can't lose her. She's all I have left, Emily. I can't."

The tears I've been holding back for so long start to spill over. I wipe them away quickly, but I know she sees them. I know she sees me breaking.

"I didn't want to tell you," I continue, my voice cracking. "I didn't want anyone to know. I don't want anyone to look at me and feel sorry for me. I don't want her to know. I can't let her know what he's done to me."

Emily's eyes soften, and before I can push her away, she's standing right in front of me, pulling me into her arms. I stiffen at first, not knowing what to do, but then I crack. I let myself sink into her, just for a moment. Just long enough to feel like someone cares.

"You're not alone, Sam," she whispers, her voice filled with more conviction than I've ever heard. "You don't have to carry this by yourself. You don't have to hide from the truth anymore."

I shake my head, the words stuck in my throat. "I don't know how to stop. I don't know how to fix this."

Emily pulls back just enough to look me in the eye. "You don't have to fix it all alone. You don't have to do it by yourself. We'll get rid of him. He doesn't deserve to be in your life. And I won't let him hurt you anymore."

Her words hit me like a ton of bricks. I want to believe her. I want to trust her, but it's hard. It's so hard. I've been alone for so long, and the idea of actually letting someone help... it scares me.

"You'll help me?" I ask, the words barely leaving my lips. "You'll help me get rid of him?"

"I will," she says, her voice steady and sure. "We'll do it together. He doesn't get to control you. He doesn't get to hurt you. You don't deserve this, Sam. And neither does your mom."

For the first time in years, I feel a spark of something I haven't felt in so long—hope. Maybe I don't have to carry this alone. Maybe Emily's right.

"I'm not alone?" I whisper, the words tasting foreign on my tongue.

"No," Emily says, her grip on my shoulders tightening. "You're not alone anymore. And I'll help you make sure he never hurts anyone again."

And for the first time, I believe her. I believe that maybe, just maybe, I don't have to hide anymore.

Chapter 7: Breaking the Silence

Samantha "Sam" Miller

The next day, I find myself sitting in the park, not knowing what to do with all these tangled emotions. It feels like everything in my life is falling apart, but it's also the first time I've felt like I can breathe since I talked to Emily yesterday.

Emily. She actually listens. And not like the other people in my life. She's not trying to fix me or tell me what to do. She's just... there. Offering her help, her understanding. It makes my skin crawl and my heart ache at the same time.

I hate feeling weak. I hate feeling like I need someone. I've lived too long thinking I didn't need anyone—thinking I was fine on my own. But yesterday, when Emily held me, I realized I've never felt so... not alone in my life.

And now I need to tell her. I need to tell her everything.

I'm pacing back and forth, my shoes crunching over the dead leaves scattered across the grass. My heart is hammering in my chest, but I force myself to sit down on the cold bench when I see Emily walking toward me. She smiles at me, but there's still something guarded in her eyes. She's waiting. Waiting for me to speak.

"Sam," she says quietly, sitting next to me. Her tone is gentle, like she already knows what I'm about to say.

I don't know where to begin. There's so much to explain. So many things I've kept locked up for years.

"Emily, I... I don't know how to do this," I mutter, trying to collect my thoughts. "I never wanted to tell you. I didn't want anyone to know. But I can't keep pretending anymore."

She doesn't push me. She just waits.

"I—I don't even know how it started," I continue, staring down at my hands. "It feels like it's always been there. But the first time... the first time was in middle school. It started slow, just little things at first, you know? But after a while, it got worse. And I didn't know how to stop it. I didn't know what to do." I take a deep breath, trying to steady my shaking hands. "I've been so stupid, Emily. I let him do that to me, to my life. And now... I can't tell my mom. I can't."

Emily doesn't interrupt, but I feel her eyes on me, watching me closely, as if trying to piece everything together.

"Why not?" she asks softly, almost like she already knows the answer.

"Because... because he's the only one she loves. He's the only one who's been there for her. If I tell her, if she finds out what he's been doing, she'll blame me. She'll say it's my fault. She'll hate me for it." My voice cracks, but I force the words out. "I'll lose her, Emily. I can't lose her. She's all I have."

A long silence stretches between us, and for a moment, I wonder if I've said too much. If she'll think I'm pathetic, weak.

But Emily doesn't pull away. She doesn't judge me. She just leans closer, her voice steady and calm.

"You're wrong, Sam," she says, her eyes unwavering. "You're wrong if you think your mom would ever blame you for this. You're wrong if you think she'd choose him over you."

I shake my head, the words bubbling up before I can stop them. "You don't get it. He's the only thing that makes her happy. She's been alone for so long. She needs him."

"She needs *you*, Sam," Emily interrupts, her tone fierce, not letting me back down. "She's your mother. And any decent mother would never choose a man over her daughter. He's not more important than you. Not now, not ever."

I can feel the weight of her words settling on my chest, but I'm still not convinced. I've seen the way she looks at him, the way she needs him to stay.

"It's not that easy," I mutter, my voice bitter. "It's not just about breaking up with him. It's not a simple fix. He's not the kind of person you can just walk away from."

Emily's face hardens, and she leans forward, her voice lowering, filled with conviction.

"No," she says, "It's not about breaking up with him. It's about getting rid of him. He needs to go to jail, Sam. He deserves to be locked away. And I'm going to help you make sure that happens."

32

I blink at her, the words hitting me harder than I expected. "What are you talking about?"

"I'm talking about making sure he can never hurt you again. Or anyone else. You're not alone in this, Sam. You don't have to keep carrying this burden by yourself."

I swallow hard, trying to keep my emotions in check. "How? How can we make sure he goes to jail? I don't even know where to start."

Emily reaches out, her hand gently touching mine. "We'll do it together. We'll find a way. We'll gather evidence, we'll talk to the right people. We'll make sure everyone knows what he's been doing. He's a monster, Sam. And monsters don't get to win."

For a moment, I just stare at her, trying to process the enormity of what she's saying. I've never had anyone stand up for me like this before. Never. It's terrifying, but it's also the first time in years that I've felt like maybe there's a way out.

"You really mean it?" I ask, barely believing the words. "You'll help me do this?"

"I swear," Emily says, her voice firm. "I'm not leaving you to fight this alone. You don't have to protect him anymore, Sam. You don't have to protect anyone but yourself."

For the first time in a long time, I feel like I'm not fighting this battle on my own. I feel like I have someone who actually *cares* about what happens to me. And for the first time, I'm starting to

33

believe that maybe—just maybe—I don't have to keep quiet anymore.

Chapter 8: The Plan

Emily Turner

I can feel the heat of the sun on my skin as I sit across from Sam in the park, her eyes locked onto mine with a mix of confusion, suspicion, and something else—maybe hope. I can't blame her for not understanding what I'm suggesting. I'm not entirely sure I understand it myself. But it's the only way. It's the only way I can think of to make sure he doesn't hurt her again.

Because Sam's right about one thing: the world won't believe her. It's a cruel reality. Women are blamed for everything. For being too quiet, too loud, too trusting, too suspicious. They'll call her a liar. They'll say she's making it up, trying to get attention. Even if she told her mother, even if she screamed it from the rooftops, it wouldn't be enough. Not unless there's evidence. Not unless we can prove it beyond a shadow of a doubt.

And that's why we need more than just her word. We need to get him. We need to catch him red-handed. There's only one way I can think of to do that—one way that'll put an end to this once and for all.

I take a deep breath and look Sam in the eyes. She's waiting for me to say something, and I know what I'm about to suggest will sound insane. Well, it *is* insane. But it's the only shot we have.

"Sam," I begin, my voice steady, "we need to set a trap. A honey trap."

Her brows furrow, her confusion palpable. "What is a honey trap?"

I can't help but feel a little guilty as I watch her process the words. But I keep going, my tone firm, my mind already running through the steps in my head.

"We need to bait him. Make him think you're vulnerable, that you're interested. Let him take the bait." I pause, letting the weight of my words settle on her. "We'll film it. When we have enough footage—when we have enough proof—we'll call the cops. They'll bust him. He'll go to jail, Sam. For good."

I can see her eyes widen, her mouth parting as if she's about to protest. But I'm not finished. I can't let her interrupt me yet.

"Think about it, Sam. This isn't just about you anymore. It's about everyone else he could hurt. The law is already stacked against you as a woman. If we don't get this on camera, if we don't have solid evidence, they'll bury this. They'll say it's a mistake or a misunderstanding. They'll blame you."

I can see her mouth tighten as I say the last words, her anger flaring up. She's not wrong, and it stings me to say it out loud, but it's the truth. It's how the world works. And that's exactly why we need to make sure there's no way for him to deny it. No way for anyone to say it didn't happen.

Sam doesn't speak for a moment. She just stares at me, and I wonder if she's going to back out. Wonder if she'll decide she can't go through with it.

But then she exhales slowly, her gaze hardening, and something shifts in her. I can see it in her eyes. She's made up her mind.

"You're really suggesting this," she says quietly, her voice barely above a whisper.

I nod. "It's the only way, Sam. We do whatever it takes to protect the people we love. And we can't afford to leave anything to chance."

She stares at me for another moment, and I can see the weight of the decision pressing down on her. She's not the same person I knew back in middle school. She's someone stronger now. Someone who's been through a lot and is willing to do anything to protect herself and the people she loves.

And when she speaks again, her voice is steady, but I can hear the crack in it. The vulnerability. She's scared, but she's also ready. She's ready to fight.

"I don't know how to do this," she says quietly. "I've never done anything like this before."

"You don't have to," I reply. "I'll be there every step of the way. We'll figure it out together."

Her eyes flick to the ground, her fingers playing with the edge of her sleeve. And then she looks up at me, her face more determined than I've ever seen it.

"I can't believe you're the one telling me this," she mutters, almost to herself. "You're so... innocent, Em. You don't even know what you're asking me to do."

I lean forward, making sure she sees the seriousness in my eyes. "I know exactly what I'm asking you to do, Sam. And you can hate me for it. You can blame me if it goes wrong. But we're going to make sure he can't hurt you anymore. We're going to make sure he never gets the chance to hurt anyone else."

For a second, I think she's going to back out. I think she's going to tell me I'm insane. But instead, she stands up, brushing off her jeans like she's shaking off the fear.

"Okay," she says, her voice low but filled with determination. "Let's do it. I'll set it up."

I smile, a little relieved but also filled with a sense of purpose. "Good. We do this together, Sam. You're not alone in this anymore."

She nods, but I can still see the hesitation in her. I know she's worried about how she's going to pull it off, but I have a plan for that too.

"I'll place the nanny cam Mom bought when we were little and use to play detective with it," I tell her. "We'll use it to record everything. He won't suspect a thing."

Sam blinks at me, processing the idea, and then nods slowly.

"And don't worry," I add. "I'll be nearby, behind the tree. I can see everything from there. If anything gets worse, I'll ring the doorbell or call for help. I won't let you suffer, Sam. I'll be there. We'll end this together."

For the first time since we started talking about this, I see a flicker of relief in her expression. The weight isn't entirely gone, but it's lighter now. She's not alone in this.

"We'll trap him," I say quietly, more to myself than to her. "And then we'll make him pay."

Sam looks at me, and for the first time in a long while, I see a flicker of hope in her eyes.

"Let's make sure he never hurts anyone again," she says.

And I know, in that moment, that we're in this together. No matter what.

Chapter 9: The Trap

Emily Turner

The day has come. The plan is in motion. Sam and I stand in my room, going over the final details. It feels surreal, like we're living in a movie, but this is real. This is happening. I'm going to help Sam take down the man who's been abusing her for years.

She stands in front of my mirror, adjusting the tight, revealing top she's wearing. She pulls at the fabric, uncomfortable, but we both know this is part of the plan. It's about making him feel like he's in control, making him believe he can have whatever he wants. But the truth? He's not in control anymore.

"Are you sure about this?" I ask, my hands trembling slightly.

Sam nods, her expression unreadable. "We're doing this. He's not getting away with it."

I try to smile, but I don't know if either of us truly believes it. This isn't something we ever imagined doing. But we don't have a choice.

Sam exhales sharply before stepping out of my room. I watch as she lets her hair fall down, straightening up, slipping into the role she once played so well—the confident girl who commanded attention, who made people fear her. But this isn't the same. This time, she's walking straight into danger.

I follow her down the hall, just long enough to activate the nanny cam we hid earlier in the living room. The small device is tucked discreetly on a shelf, perfectly positioned to capture everything. We tested the feed—it's working. As soon as the camera is live, I grab my phone and slip out the back door, hurrying to my hiding spot behind the tree, where I can watch everything unfold on my screen.

The video feed is crisp, streaming the scene inside in real time. The room looks the same as always—too normal for what's about to happen. He's sitting on the couch, flipping through old magazines like he doesn't have a care in the world.

Then Sam steps into view.

I see the way he looks at her. His gaze lingers, predatory and calculating. My stomach twists with rage, but I keep still, watching.

She moves toward him, brushing past him just enough to make it seem natural, like a girl seeking attention. His lips curl into a knowing smirk.

"What's the matter, kid? You wanna play? I've got time," he says, his voice thick with intent.

Sam doesn't flinch. "Tell me exactly what you're going to do to me," she says, her voice steady, challenging him.

He chuckles, leaning forward. "Oh, you want to know? I'll show you exactly what I'm going to do. I'll take you… wherever I want."

That's all I need. I've already got 911 dialed, whispering into the phone as I give them the address. But we didn't account for what happens next.

Instead of just talking, instead of playing along with the bait, he grabs her wrist. Hard.

My heart stops.

Sam stiffens, and for the first time, I see real fear in her eyes.

I clutch my phone, fingers tightening around it. This wasn't part of the plan.

He yanks her toward him, his grip unrelenting. "You think you can just tease me, huh?" His voice drops lower, more dangerous. "You think I don't know what you're up to?"

Sam swallows hard, but then—she smiles. It's small, teasing, just enough to keep him hooked. "You always say I'm worth the wait," she murmurs. "Don't you want it to be perfect?"

He doesn't let go. Instead, his grip tightens.

Sam's smile falters for just a second—just long enough for him to notice. His smirk widens. He leans in, his breath heavy with cigarettes and whiskey, the scent suffocating.

"You think you're in control?" he murmurs, his fingers sliding up her arm, squeezing tight enough to leave marks. "You think I don't see right through you? You came here for a reason, baby. And it sure as hell wasn't to talk."

I can barely breathe.

The phone is shaking in my hand, but I force myself to stay silent. Stay still. Keep recording.

Sam, unbelievably, doesn't pull away. She doesn't scream. She doesn't fight. Instead, she tilts her head, keeping that same teasing smirk on her lips, her voice barely above a whisper.

"You're right," she breathes. "I came here because I wanted to. Because I missed you."

His eyes darken, hunger flashing across his face. He drags her closer, pressing his body against hers.

"You missed me?" he echoes, his voice thick with amusement. "That's not what you said last time. You begged me to leave you alone, remember?"

Sam lets out a soft, breathy laugh. "I was scared. I didn't understand back then." She tilts her head just slightly, exposing the curve of her neck. "But I do now. You taught me."

His breathing grows heavier. His fingers creep down her arm, slow and possessive.

"That's right," he whispers. "I did teach you, didn't I? You were such a little brat at first—always running away, acting like you were better than me. But you learned, didn't you?"

Sam's lips part, her voice still steady, coaxing. "Tell me how. Tell me everything. I wanna hear it."

He laughs softly, his thumb tracing the inside of her wrist. "You want me to remind you?" His voice drops lower, almost gentle. "I made you mine. I broke you in. No matter how much you screamed, no matter how much you cried, I knew you'd come back. Because deep down, you liked it."

My stomach churns. I feel sick.

Sam doesn't flinch. She doesn't waver. She lets him talk, lets him confess.

He tightens his grip on her waist, his other hand creeping toward her thigh. "I was good to you," he whispers. "I made you feel special. And now, you're finally ready for more, aren't you?"

She exhales, a shiver running down her spine. But her voice stays firm. "Yes," she murmurs. "But not here. Somewhere private."

His fingers dig in. His mouth moves toward her ear.

I see the sick pleasure in his eyes.

He's going to take her.

My heart is pounding. Come on, come on, hurry up.

Then—

On my screen, I see movement outside—red and blue lights flashing.

They're here.

Sam holds his gaze, keeping up the act. "Not here," she whispers. "Let's go somewhere else. Somewhere private."

The door bursts open.

Two officers rush in.

One of them tackles him to the floor, pinning him down before he can even react. The other reaches for Sam, steadying her as she stumbles back, shaking.

I exhale, my whole body trembling. It's over.

I step out from behind the tree just as Sam looks up and sees me. Tears brim in her eyes. "Did we... did we really do it?"

I nod, my throat tight.

The officer holding him down yanks his arms behind his back, locking the cuffs. "You're done," he growls. "You're never touching another girl again."

They haul him up, leading him toward the door.

Sam wipes at her eyes, her voice barely a whisper. "Thank you."

I grip her hand. "You don't have to thank me. You're my friend. And I'll do whatever it takes to protect you."

We watch as they take him away, disappearing into the night.

I exhale, my chest feeling lighter than it has in days.

Sam is free.

And for the first time, she's not alone.

Chapter 10: The Truth Comes Out

Emily Turner

The air in the house feels different now. Lighter, but heavy with the weight of everything that has happened. I can hear the front door open as Sam's mother steps inside, her voice muffled at first as she talks to someone. The officers, still talking among themselves in the living room, have left, but the tension remains. The reality of what we've done, what we've stopped, is settling in.

Sam's mother walks into the living room, her eyes immediately locking on Sam. I can see the storm brewing in her gaze. She doesn't need to ask what happened—she knows. She can feel the shift in the air, the change. She can tell her daughter is no longer the same girl who walked out this morning, who was afraid and broken.

"What did you do?" Sam's mom asks, her voice wavering between confusion and anger.

Sam stands there, her body stiff, her face pale. She's not sure how to answer. I can see it in her eyes—she's scared. But it's not the same fear she's always had. This fear is different. This is the fear of being seen, of letting the truth out.

"I... I didn't want you to know," Sam says quietly. Her voice cracks as the weight of her secret comes pouring out. "I didn't want to lose you."

Her mother steps forward, her face softening. "Sam... why didn't you tell me? Why didn't you come to me?"

Sam looks down, her hands trembling at her sides. "I thought... I thought if you knew, you'd hate me. I thought if you knew what he was doing, you'd blame me. I thought you'd... leave me."

The words hit Sam's mother like a punch to the gut. I watch as she takes a shaky breath, the tears gathering in her eyes as she looks at her daughter. "No, baby," she says softly, her voice breaking. "You're my daughter. I would never blame you. Never."

Her mother steps forward and pulls Sam into a tight embrace, her arms wrapping around her as though trying to hold on to her as if she might slip away. "I'm so sorry. I should've seen it. I should've known. I should've been there for you."

Sam's body shakes as she lets out a sob, her arms wrapping around her mother in return. "I was afraid you'd choose him over me," Sam whispers through her tears.

Her mother pulls back slightly, wiping her daughter's tears away with the back of her hand. "I was wrong. I was blind. Nothing, *nothing* is more important than you, Sam. You are everything to me. You always have been. I'm so sorry for not being there sooner. But I'm here now, and I will never let him hurt you again."

I watch as they hold each other, the two of them finally understanding how deeply they needed each other all along. There's a new understanding between them, a new bond that was broken for too long but is slowly being mended.

I stand back, not wanting to intrude, but Sam's eyes find mine. She steps away from her mother for a moment, her face still streaked with tears, but there's something different about her now. Something softer, more vulnerable, yet stronger too.

"Emily... I—" Sam starts, her voice faltering. "I don't know how to thank you for what you did. I was so angry at you for so long, but... you saved me."

I shake my head, walking over to her. "You don't need to thank me. You didn't need saving, Sam. You just needed to be heard. You needed to know you weren't alone. And now, you know that."

Sam nods slowly, wiping her eyes with the back of her hand. "I... I don't know what would've happened if you hadn't been there. I don't know if I could've ever told anyone... I don't think I could've."

"You would have," I say, my voice steady, but inside, I can feel the lump in my throat. "You just needed someone to help you see it wasn't your fault. That you didn't have to carry it alone."

Sam looks at me, her face full of gratitude, but also something deeper. Something I didn't expect. "I was so lost, Emily. I didn't know what to do. I was so scared. But now... I don't know if I'll ever be the same."

I smile softly, stepping closer to her. "You won't be the same. But that's okay. We're never the same after something like this. But you'll be stronger. You'll be more whole than you ever were before."

Sam nods slowly, her face softening with understanding. "I'm sorry for everything... for how I treated you. For all the times I made you feel like crap. I was... I was hurting and I didn't know how to handle it."

"It's okay," I reply, reaching out to place a hand on her arm. "You don't need to apologize for that. We're both different now. We're both stronger."

"I can't believe how much you've helped me. I never thought I'd ever feel safe again. But now... I don't feel alone."

"You're not alone," I tell her firmly. "You never have been. And we won't let you be again."

Sam looks at me, her eyes bright with a mixture of relief and hope. "I don't know how to move forward from all of this."

"You move forward by knowing that nothing gets fixed unless you do it yourself," I say, my voice low but full of conviction. "You can't change the past, Sam. You can't take back the time you've lost. But you can take control of the future. And you're doing that now. You're taking back your life. And I'll be here every step of the way."

Sam smiles, a real smile this time, one that reaches her eyes. "Thank you, Emily. I never thought I'd be saying that, but... thank you."

I smile back at her. "No need to thank me. This is us. We're in this together now."

Her mother steps forward, placing a hand on Sam's shoulder, her eyes full of pride and love. "You've got each other now. And nothing can take that away."

We all stand there for a moment, a family—two broken souls, finding their way back to each other, ready to rebuild what had been torn apart.

Nothing gets fixed unless you do it yourself. But together, we'll make sure nothing gets broken again.

The End.